# (re)memory

Kayleen Hedberg

BookLeaf Publishing
India | USA | UK

Presentation by *BookLeaf Publishing*

Web: www.bookleafpub.com

E-mail: info@bookleafpub.com

ISBN: 9789357448598

First edition 2022

# DEDICATION

for the forgotten

# ACKNOWLEDGEMENT

I thank my family and my friends from the bottom of my heart for watering me in times of withering and in times of growth. Thank you for remembering who I am when I have forgotten. Thank you for leaving space for me to remember. Thank you for leaving space for me to forget. Thank you for showing me that I am more than a memory. Thank you for showing me that I am enough.

A special thank you to BookLeaf Publishing for building a home for my words to rest – they are glad to be alive, here.

# PREFACE

Your memory is a monster; you forget – it doesn't. It simply files things away. It keeps things for you, or hides things from you – and summons them to your recall with a will of its own. You think you have a memory; but it has you!

– John Irving

# it bleeds from with(in)

i walk down the brick steps and lower my head as i pass under the archway. a metal door emerges, barred like a prison. i have been here before, in a memory. a table through the door seats a clipboard and a pen, and i sign myself in. he appears on my left and holds his palm out to me, facing up. i plunge the pen into his palm. he thanks me, and leaves.

# sharing is (s)caring

it's the little changes, and the big ones.

once i walked in the sunlight to read aloud my own words to a room full of people. it was cold that day, but the warm kind of cold.

you know the one i mean; the kind where your toes curl in the slush but the sun asks you to shed your coat anyway.

over a hundred people heard my words, but i never did. it's funny how sometimes our best memories are a little empty.

i don't remember what happened or how it went, but i remember it made me happy.

my memory isn't what it used to be, but i don't really know if it ever actually used to be at all, anyway.

a leaf curled in my hair the other day and made itself at home in the tangled strings.

i remember that. i remember that.

# i am still (search)ing for me

the ship bobs softly in the water, dark and looming. the mast is chipped and the captain wears a wicked smile. at the back of the boat, a girl rummages through a pile of mirrors. how do i know which one is me? she says.

# i hope it's (ok)ay but

it came in shades of gray and gold, like bursts of stars against her eyes. on a frozen night in november when gravity pulled crispened leaves from their branches she sat on the tracks and wept. it was cold. her breath left her in little puffs of white, her sanity escaping with each cloud. from the distance she heard the cackling. a siren, a sycamore, an amulet, a sneeze. flash after flash the pain came, each sting dazzling her. okay, she whimpered. okay.

# i could have (die)d

i see things like people around me.

they come to me and whisper about accidents

and times when i almost died but didn't.

the thing about traumatic brain injury is that it takes

away your bravery, your balance, your bustle, but also

your memory.

and if your memory isn't there anymore,

you're erased. you're gone. right?

so these things surround me.

and i'm tired of ignoring them, you know?

foolish girl, you died years ago.

# moving on is im(possible)

before i was born, i was in a tank with a leopard who had rice for teeth.

we spent our days together, the leopard and i, and when people passed us by we fanned our arms like fins. sometimes i seek the comfort of the asleep, but even in my dreams i return to my leopard, or my leopard returns to me.

we return to our tank, but we have grown so much that only our heads fit anymore. we practice fanning our arms as my leopard's teeth cook in the tank water. my leopard tells me i was not born to sleep and that when i awake i will have trouble finding our tank again. when i am awake, i find our tank in unlikely places, the curtains, the closet, the kitchen, but my leopard is gone.

i sleep, i sleep.

# should i always (mis)trust a gift

there was a man who stole shadows from the town. he snatched them from alleyway meetings and planted them in his greenhouse at home. he would water them at daybreak and enrich the soil with canned screams. this continued for weeks and weeks until one day, the mother returned. i brought you a gift, she said, and handed him a bucket of purple smoke. it's for the shadows, she explained. the man took the bucket and strode to his greenhouse. he reached in and scooped a handful of the purple smoke, gently sprinkling it over his shadows. one by one, his shadows reformed into bodies and by daybreak, the man was sprawled on the floor of his greenhouse.

# appoint //
# (dis)appoint

it smelled like a bookshop in my dream. a second baseman called me from the field and asked me to challenge a call, but i couldn't do it. he said, they're disappointed in you, and i could hear through the crowd that he was right. on a train ride through stamford i watched a nanny take a bag of crackers from the toddler next to her and i wrote in my journal: the thing we have in common is that we disappoint, we disappoint.

# be(longing) is an interesting concept

i miss this dog that wasn't even mine.

we were there for my brother to adopt a grizzly and we passed a crate with a dog that cowered inside. i can't remember his name. he looked like a fox.

anyways, the dog cowered inside and my heart tugged for this fearful guy. an associate at the shelter opened the fox's crate but he wouldn't come near anybody. but he came to me.

i took him to the visitation room and sat with him, pet him, spoke to him. the way this dog looked at me, it was like he was looking into my soul and telling me that he was mine and i was his, and it was time to go home now, okay? but i couldn't afford him.

i will never forget the way he looked when we took him back to his crate. he sat right at the

front now, staring at me and staring at me and
staring at me.

i miss this dog that wasn't even mine. i got him
to trust me and i left him behind.

# (every)thing fragile will break

you remind me of a poem, he said. it was light
outside now, and the violets with their frosted
petals warmed in the rising sun.

let's paint a window on the wall and call it glass,
i said.

what if it breaks? he said.

then we have our very own dear telescope, i
said.

we harvested sun until our hands scooped space
and we burned like madness in a jar.

# one orange split to-(go)

what do a wedding band and an orange have in common?

they're both circles. they both have a relationship to skin. they're both made of warm colors. warm. warmth. when you peel an orange do you peel it like the band, how both reveal something smothered underneath? they can both be pulled out and put away. should you put a wedding band in a pantry? i forget.

what do a wedding band and an orange have in common? it makes me feel suffocated and i guess if i was allergic to oranges i would feel suffocated too.

# it was me all a(long)

the shadows chased me until i sprawled, bloody,
at their feet. they spoke to me of a hidden dagger
entrusted to the wrong reaper, the one assigned
to me. stop running from us, they said. we're
trying to help you. i could see they were sincere
and as they pled for me to listen i succumbed to
the shadows. they carried me through a terrain
that was unknown to me, but i didn't care – it
just felt so nice to be carried. they carried me
and carried me and carried me. the last thing i
remember is something that glinted of silver. it
was strange though. i think i held it in my hands.

# w(he)n ptsd meets a mirror

i saw something in the mirror, disappearing lines
like dripping candle wax or a stifled guffaw
from the nighttime. when i looked closer i saw
the lines were bloody, like the scars around my
mouth from the accident. it couldn't have been a
flashback – those were for times of
inconvenience. this was something else.

i think it was a ghost.
sorry, i always forget.
i think it is a ghost.

# i think (stay)ing would be silly

a necklace for a giant would be a silly thing.

but so would a lot of things, like me leaving or me staying or me.

# i should stop (hold)ing onto 2011

i dreamt of a flower last night, like a name or a memory of you. it crept under my eyelids in the moonlight and made me cry, dampening my pillow and my hair and my face. it didn't last long, or at least not long enough, and when i awoke i made tea and cried again. in the dream you were blue and smelled like the last evening before winter, like frost and decay. you were holding a note from 2011 and when i stole it from your grasp it disintegrated before my eyes, my hollow, my wet, wet eyes.

# when i dis(cover) myself

he places the coffee thermos on the table and i
move to pick it up, but discover that i can't.
when i look down at my hands, they have been
replaced by my feet. i look up at him,
embarrassed, but he isn't paying attention. i
lower my feet to my lap and pretend i don't want
the coffee. i like the color of your nails, he says.

# in which they are inter(view)ed

she walked alone.

by alone, we mean that there were no others present.

does this satisfy the committee?

hey, a riddle for you: what has three doubles in one?

sorry, we thought it was original.

yes, of course, back to her. she walked alone.

no, we believe it was by choice.

personals? i mean… we discovered she carried a small something –

we don't know how to get more specific, we're sorry.

describe it? well – it was small.

she held it in her hand and kept rubbing her
thumb over the back of it.

maybe it was a piece broken off of a whole. like
we said – it was small.

she looked bruised, if we're being honest.

no, some of them were old. but others were
fresh.

look: we know better than to question the
committee. but who is this girl?

# it comes in wave(s)

sometimes in the middle of a dance the floor will collapse and i'll remember the math problem i could never quite solve, or maybe it was science, or maybe it was life.

# w(here) i come from

this disease of mine, it's something else. there
are worms in my brain, digging deeper and
deeper and deeper, slithering away from an
unseen robin on the prowl. my first therapist
once said i'm the bird in this scenario, and it's
my responsibility to pluck the worms from their
gray matter tunnels. i didn't go back to her. i
don't like clutter. if there was a way to take the
worms out, i would.

do you think the ground remembers what it was
like to grow? i see houses covering what used to
be corn fields filled with little brown bugs that
were impossible to kill on a bathroom floor.
maybe their armor was so they would never
forget where they came from. if memory comes
from the mind, and my mind is filled with
worms and disease and decay, how can i trust
that anything i remember belongs to me?

once, i rushed to the edge of a cliff to catch a hat
flying in the wind. it was a few years before i cut
out a life that held me back.

if memories come flooding back, they must be in
the form of water. it makes sense, i suppose,
how i used to feel so cleansed by them, how now
i'm drowning, drowning, drowning.

warm tears leak out the corners of my eyes and
all i can think is that i vaguely taste mustard.

# (re)member

i have to be a member
again
and again
and again.

they never asked me if it's what i wanted.
how could they have found the time, with all of
the sleeping?

sleep is a weird thing. you're alive but you're
unaware.
does that mean that to sleep is to be ignorant?
when someone dies they call it the eternal sleep.
or sometimes people say: you can sleep when
you're dead.
that's always a weird one, to me. sleep is an
action of the living.
in movies when someone dies,
they close the eyelids and say: there. they might
as well be sleeping.

we can accept sleep more than we can accept
death, but when you're sleeping you have to
wake up and be a member again and again and

again and they never asked me if it's what i
wanted.

24

# intentions are
# c(heap)

i didn't mean to drink so much poetry but then
the words fell out of me and i sit here scrubbing
them off the bathroom floor hoping hoping
hoping it'll never stop.